WILLIAM DEAL

GOD'S ANSWER FOR THE
UNEQUALLY YOKED

GOOD NEWS PUBLISHERS
WESTCHESTER, ILLINOIS

Library of Congress Catalog Card Number 80-67387
ISBN 0-89107-182-2

*To that noble host of Christians who
are unequally yoked in marriage to unbelievers,
and who must continually cope with the problems
such a marriage brings, this book is
lovingly dedicated.*

Contents

Preface 9

1. Facing the Issue 11

2. Understanding Christian Commitment 17

3. God's Guidelines for the Husband 25

4. God's Guidelines for the Wife 41

5. Going the Second Mile 65

6. Building a Bridge to Tomorrow 75

Notes 89

Preface

Upon the urgent requests of pastors needing book-length material on the unequally yoked marriage, I began writing this volume and researching whatever helps I could find. The book includes references to other materials available on the topic.

I have attempted to deal honestly with the subject, even when it has meant being brutally honest with the unbelieving mate who refuses to receive Christ as Savior and follow his teachings. But I have also made a definite plea in behalf of the unconverted spouse. Only when a husband and wife experience unity in Christ can they enjoy marriage at its best. I pray that this book will help many couples move toward that end.

As a former pastor, district superintendent of schools, and college president, I have had opportunity to observe hundreds of Christians and their marriage relationships. There seem to me to be far more Christian wives than Christian husbands. Hence, this book deals mainly with the matter of how to cope with the unsaved husband and less often with the matter of the Christian man married to an unsaved wife.

The first purpose of this book is admittedly to help the Christian spouse live the victorious Christian life despite the handicaps and difficulties encountered in a marriage to an unsaved mate. But a second purpose is to help the unsaved spouse see the need to receive Christ as Savior, thus finding happiness and fulfillment in life and putting his or her marriage on a much stronger base. The Bible has much to say about the institution of marriage. It is indeed a *marriage manual,* to which this book is secondary.

I invite both husband and wife, whether Christian or not, to read this book carefully. No matter what your present spiritual attitude, you will find material in this book that will be particularly helpful to you personally. May God bless you as you seek his guidance in making needed adjustments in your marriage.

1
Facing the Issue

Can two walk together, except they be agreed?
(Amos 3:3)

"And whosoever doth not bear his cross, and come
after me, cannot be my disciple." (Luke 14:27)

For he hath said, I will never leave thee, nor forsake thee. So that we may boldly say, The Lord is
my helper, and I will not fear what man shall do
unto me. (Hebrews 13:5, 6)

As a young single pastor I had a startling intro-
duction to the marital problems involved in living the Christian life before an unsaved marriage partner. I boarded in the home of one of
my church members, my room being directly
over the bedroom of my Christian friend. On a
Saturday morning, not long after I began living
in the house, I heard a commotion coming from
downstairs. A moment later I heard my friend's
wife shout furiously, "I'll kick you out of this
bed, you blue-eyed devil!"

Shocked into attention, I heard my friend's kind, gentle reply, almost inaudible to me. My heart settled down from its rapid beat. I knew he had the victory, spiritually, in this terrible situation.

For many years this godly man lived with this unconverted woman, staying true to Christ and maintaining a good Christian witness in his community. Probably the entire populace of the little town in which he lived would have stood up for him, and even fought for him if necessary. Everyone who knew him had confidence in his Christian life and testimony.

How did he manage to live so successfully with his ungodly wife? She seldom attended church and had no interest in religion—except when she thought she was going to die! She was of little or no help in giving their children a Christian upbringing. She seemed to enjoy giving him a rough time in every way she could. What was his secret of living victoriously in Christ? The work of Jesus Christ in his life was the answer for him, and is for you.

I am happy to say that this man's prayers and faithful witness paid off. Several years ago, his wife turned to God and was saved, just a few weeks before she died. Who knows how much his faithfulness to God and to his marriage helped her to finally come to the Savior.

A godly woman of my acquaintance lived a long and successful life with an ungodly husband. He took no interest in religion and made fun of her friends, her minister, her church. What was her secret of radiant Christian living? God's work within one of his children was what accomplished this.

Many dedicated Christians have unsaved mates. This is usually because of a wife or husband becoming a Christian after the marriage ceremony, while the spouse remains an unbeliever.

It is not my desire to insult or injure any unbeliever married to a Christian husband or wife. I have empathy for the unsaved companion of a faithful Christian. But the true Christian cannot compromise his convictions or lower his Christian standards and still live before God victoriously, expecting his blessing. The non-Christian, not having been born of the Spirit, cannot live the Christian life. This is bound to bring friction at times despite anything the Christian in the unequal marriage can do. Even if the unbelieving mate lives a moral life and does not indulge in excessive or open sinful practices, his life and ways are going to be at cross-purposes with the believer's.

There are many things in the entertainment world which unbelievers enjoy and want their companions to enjoy with them. But Christians have no interest in many of these amusements and, in fact, *cannot* enjoy them. The believer may feel that to attend some of these places would compromise his Christian witness and bring dishonor to his Lord. If the unsaved husband must go to questionable sites alone, he often does not enjoy himself. Or if the unsaved wife finds her husband will not go with her to undesirable places, she may feel hurt, ostracized, unhappy. If she is compelled to give up these outside social activities, she may feel she is a victim of unfairness or even cruelty.

It must be possible to successfully live the Christian life within an unequal marriage: to know what to do and what not to do; to live Christianly and yet not disrupt the harmony of the home where one marriage partner is an unbeliever.

Jesus taught, "Ye are the light of the world. A city that is set on an hill cannot be hidden. Neither do men light a lamp, and put it under a bushel, but on a lampstand, and it giveth light unto all that are in the house. Let your light so shine before men, that they may see your good works, and glorify your Father, who is in heaven" (Matthew 5:14-16).

In order to fully analyze these matters, it will be necessary to examine the Christian cause—at least in a general way. We must see what Christ demands of his followers, what he expects of them in daily living. We must also explore how far the marriage covenant binds the Christian to the unbeliever and what the unbeliever's rights are in such a union.

Both the Christian and the unbeliever should reserve judgment on this book's message until they have read it through and fully understand its content. All Scripture references should be examined carefully. In this way, both the husband and wife may gain clearer focus on Christ and the life he has given to the believer.

2
Understanding Christian Commitment

"If any man come to me, and hate not his father, and mother, and wife, and children, and brethren, and sisters, yea, and his own life also, he cannot be my disciple." (Luke 14:26)

In order to better understand the relationship between the Christian and an unbelieving mate, it is first necessary to comprehend what is involved in the Christian's commitment to Christ. There is nothing to be gained in trying to hide one's Christian faith; this only confuses the issue and further muddies the marital waters. If, from the beginning of the marriage or from the time of the salvation experience, the unbeliever can be helped to understand what God expects from the Christian, the couple can avoid unnecessary conflict in the marriage. The unbeliever hopefully will decide, if he cannot go along with his Christian mate, that at least he will not oppose his spouse's beliefs, nor try to change them and substitute his own unbeliefs instead. Such a neutral position on the part of the unbeliever will foster marital harmony.

The unbeliever must be helped to understand from the beginning that the Christian is not merely giving allegiance to a local church, or to an organization, or even to a set of religious beliefs, but to Jesus Christ himself. Likewise, failure to live Christianly is failure to obey Jesus Christ. What does Christ really ask of his followers?

Total Commitment to Jesus Christ

One cannot live a truly Christian life with anything less than total commitment to Christ as Savior and Lord. Being a Christian demands the giving of oneself to Christ, the bringing of body, soul, mind, and heart into full obedience to the will of God as revealed in the Old and New Testaments. The Christian is responsible to perform as much of the will of God for his life as he perceives to be God's will for him.

Christian Living—Not Merely a Sunday Affair

Christianity is a seven-days-a-week commitment to living loyally for the Lord. Certainly, the Christian makes mistakes as everyone does, but if he is spiritually perceptive, he will be eager to apologize, to accept blame for his errors, and to correct them in the future.

The new convert to Christianity may have weaknesses in his makeup that may cause him to say and do things which are not exemplary of the

Christian life. However, he learns day by day more and more lessons of truth as he depends on the Holy Spirit to teach him. These lessons are learned from the Bible, from the preaching of the Word of God by spiritual teachers, and from mature Christians whose lives influence the younger believer.

The Christian life is much like being in the armed services. A young man volunteers for service in the Army. He is sworn in, which is like conversion to Christ. Experiences in boot training may be compared to the Christian's early days of service for his Lord. There is so much to learn at first in the service, both the Lord's and Uncle Sam's.

Leaves of absence take a soldier away from his regular duties for a few days. But he is still a soldier. Should he be called to return to duty before his leave is up, he must go back at once without quibbling about his orders.

Likewise, the new Christian may experience brief times of absence from regular attendance at services, prayer, and Bible reading. But he must return to his spiritual duties when the Spirit of God convicts him about his absence. As the soldier may not be AWOL just to please some person not in the armed forces, so the Christian cannot be AWOL from his church services, Bible reading, or prayer times just to please an unbeliever, even if that unbeliever is a close loved one.

You cannot succeed in the Christian life without uncompromising loyalty to Christ, attendance when possible in the house of God, and attention to Bible reading and prayer. Total commitment is a necessity for both soldier and Christian. While a true Christian opposed by an unbelieving mate can remain true to God and skip services at times to please the unsaved one, it is not the ideal way to cope with the problem. But if he or she *must* miss services in order to keep peace in the home, God can give grace and keep the believer inwardly close to Christ in his heart and life. Faithfulness to God in the believer's heart is the most important element of Christian living. "Man looketh on the outward appearance, but the Lord looketh on the heart" (1 Samuel 16:7).

Christian Accountability

The Christian should realize that he is accountable to God for his own faith; but he must also give account to God for teaching his children God's laws and God's ways. Moses explicitly instructed his people that they were to teach their children the words God had given to Israel:

Hear, O Israel: The Lord our God is one Lord: And thou shalt love the Lord thy God with all thine heart, and with all thy soul, and with all thy might. And these words, which I command thee this day, shall be in thine heart; and thou shalt teach them diligently unto thy children, and shalt talk of them when thou sittest in thine house, and when thou walkest by the way, and when thou liest down, and when thou risest up. And thou shalt bind them for a sign upon thine hand, and they shall be as frontlets between thine eyes. And thou shalt write them upon the posts of thy house, and on thy gates.

(Deuteronomy 6:4-9)

Just as the ancient Israelite was to drill his children in the laws and concepts of God, the Christian today is obligated to teach his children the Christian walk and way, both by word and example. He is not to try to "cram religion down their throats," but rather is to teach his children from early childhood the way of Christ, the truths about salvation, and how to live the Christian life. The Apostle Paul was very definite about this:

And, ye, fathers, provoke not your children to wrath, but bring them up in the nurture and admonition of the Lord.

(Ephesians 6:4)

This training should include a daily prayer time with the children. In addition to family prayers, it is important to pray individually with each child on occasions when it is needed, and when it seems to be required in helping him to find release from some special stress or problem. John Wesley gave his praying mother credit for taking time to pray with each child, despite the demands of caring for her large family. No doubt, this special effort built character in her children's lives.

One may say, "Well, I'm not the head of the house. That is my husband's responsibility." Or,

"I leave religion to my wife as far as the children are concerned." Such excuses do not release a parent from his or her duty. The responsibility for each child's religious welfare rests squarely with *each* parent. Where one parent will not shoulder his obligation, it becomes an even greater responsibility for the Christian parent to see that the children are properly instructed. In addition to training in Sunday school on Sunday and midweek Bible classes, if available, daily instruction in the home must not be neglected. Private Christian schools are springing up because of the spiritual vacuum in public schools, and enrollment in a Christian school can be of special help to the child from a home where one parent is not a Christian.

When there is conflict in the home over child-rearing, the question arises, "How far does the husband's dominion go in the training of the children?" This is an important question and demands a well-defined answer.

We see in Genesis that God created Adam and Eve in his image and for his glory.

> And God said, Let us make man in our image, after our likeness; and let them have dominion over the fish of the sea, and over the fowl of the air, and over the cattle, and over all the earth, and over every creeping thing that creepeth upon the earth. So God created man in his own image, in the image of God created he him; male and female created he them (Genesis 1:26, 27).

They were to live in obedience to him and to

love and serve him throughout all their days. Man was to exercise dominion over creation, and this included being the head of the family.

As long as a man honors God and lives for him, he is fulfilling his position as the head of the home. As the head, he must be God-fearing, upright in all his ways, and dependable in every sense of the word. He cannot *demand* the respect and love of his wife and children; he must *earn* their love and respect by his life and conduct.

Just as every person earns his position in life by his conduct, or loses his place of honor by misconduct, so does the husband. He holds his God-given place of authority as head of the home by his loyalty to Jesus Christ and by carrying out his responsibilities. By the same token, he forfeits his position as head of the wife and of the household by rejecting God and refusing to fulfill his God-appointed responsibilities.

No Holding Back

Christ demands the Christian's total devotion and love. There can be no holding back. Just as a wife who really cares for her husband, or a husband who truly loves his wife, cannot put another love first, so the Lord demands full and complete heart-surrender, total commitment of all to him. Christ cannot be second in the Christian's life, any more than the wife or husband can take second place in the love of the other and be content. "Jesus said unto him, Thou shalt love the Lord, thy God, with all thy heart, and with all thy soul, and with all thy mind. This is the first and greatest commandment" (Matthew 22:37, 38).

There is to be nothing less than total dedication to God for the Christian, not even for the sake of the dearest one on earth in a human relationship. Such a commitment must be made if there is to be any genuine Christian living. Jesus taught this truth over and over. For example, "If any man will come after me, let him deny himself, and take up his cross daily, and follow me" (Luke 9:23). (Also see Matthew 10:38; 16:24; Mark 8:34-36.)

It may seem like doubletalk to say that in addition to the total dedication due to the Lord, the Christian has certain obligations to his or her unsaved mate. These obligations will be dealt with more fully later on, but here we want to at least say that the Lord loved that unsaved one enough to die for him or her. Though he has not yet yielded to God, God has not lost interest in him. In fact, as Paul writes to the Corinthians, "For the unbelieving husband is sanctified by the wife, and the unbelieving wife is sanctified by the husband; else were your children unclean, but now are they holy" (1 Corinthians 7:14). Here "sanctified" means "set apart for a spiritual work of grace." God wants to reach out to the unsaved marriage partner through the saved one.

3
God's Guidelines for the Husband

For the husband is the head of the wife, even as Christ is the head of the church. . . . Therefore, as the church is subject unto Christ, so let the wives be to their own husbands in everything. (Ephesians 5:23, 24)

In like manner, ye husbands, dwell with them according to knowledge, giving honor unto the wife, as unto the weaker vessel, and being heirs together of the grace of life, that your prayers be not hindered. (1 Peter 3:7)

The husband has heavy responsibilities in his home, based on requirements which the Lord himself has laid upon him. As long as the husband and father meets these divinely appointed duties, the climate of the home will be one of happiness and harmony—provided the wife is also a Christian and carries out her responsibilities. This does not mean that there will never be disruption in the smooth operation of the home, nor that the parents will never disagree or have tense discussions about issues. But it does mean that so long as the husband fulfills his responsibilities, first to God and then to his wife and children, God will prosper him and his home.

What are the God-given responsibilities of the husband and father?

When the Husband Is a Christian

The husband is to be the head of the home. Paul was very specific in setting down this guideline. "For the husband is the head of the wife, even as Christ is the head of the church; and he is the savior of the body" (Ephesians 5:23).

Dr. Clyde Narramore has well said, "God has charged man with the role of leadership. The husband has special responsibilities in the home. He has the responsibility of provision, protection, of honoring his wife, and loving her. He is the head of the home."[1]

A Christian counselor tells the story of an attorney who became a Christian, but his wife remained an unbeliever and even opposed his having family devotions with the children. Going the extra mile to please her, the husband would take the children to school, and on the way in the car he would help them memorize Scriptures and have prayer with them.

For this husband, having "car devotions" seemed to him the best he could do. However, as head of the home he should have taken a firm stand and had prayer with the children even if his wife did protest. He obviously respected his wife and did not push this matter with her. But does not the Christian have not only the right, but the responsibility to conduct devotions with the children in the home? It is a sad state of affairs when the devil, through the unsaved spouse, is allowed to take the lead and control the spiritual climate in the home.

After receiving Christ, an outstanding engineer in a large industrial company went home to face his Christless wife and worldly daughter. Together, the two unbelievers decided to put a stop to his "Christian nonsense." First, they would stay away from the table until he had said grace. This didn't deter him, so they took a new approach. They would come to the table and sit there as sullen and mean-looking as they could, giving him the silent treatment. This went on for a month or two. Then they tried striking their glasses, spoons and plates together and making all sorts of clattering sounds while he asked the blessing on the meal. The man was about to give up when one evening his wife accompanied him to church and there received Christ as her Savior. The husband shuddered to think how near he had come to spiritual shipwreck because of his family's campaign. Sticking it out paid off for him and will for you, too, Christian husband or Christian wife. Hold on faithfully to the end!

The Christian husband is responsible to obey God's first and highest commandment: "Thou shalt have no other gods before me" (Deuteronomy 5:7). Jesus summarized the Ten Commandments as follows: "Thou shalt love the Lord thy God with all thy heart, and with all thy soul, and with all thy mind, and with all thy strength: this is the first commandment. And the second is this: Thou shalt love thy neighbor as thyself. There is no other commandment greater than these" (Mark 12:30, 31). When the husband and father fulfills this first responsibility each day, he will have less difficulty fulfilling his other responsibilities. If he disobeys this one, he will not be able to really perform the others.

The husband and wife should have prayer together often for the strengthening and encouragement of each other in the Lord. Each should read the Word individually for personal growth, but they should also find a special time to read the Bible together.

When children grace the home, it becomes the father's responsibility to head up the teaching and training of these young lives in the things of God. As we saw earlier in Deuteronomy 6:4-9, God requires that parents teach their children all of his precepts and laws; that is, they are to teach, explain, and impart to them as much as they know about the ways of God and the plan of salvation. If the father absolutely cannot find time for this each day, he should encourage his wife to set aside time to instruct the children in the Word. But he should do his share of teaching and training as opportunity permits. There are many Bible games in Christian bookstores that can help to make this time of instruction a fun time. If as parents we are too busy to train our children for God, then we are too busy to be the parents God commands us to be! Dare we disobey him?

Though head of the home, the husband and father will not take undue advantage of the wife or other members of the family because of his position. He will not "bully" his family. This would violate Christ's commandment to love our neighbor as ourselves and would ignore his noble words, "Therefore, all things whatever ye would that men should do to you, do ye even so to them" (Matthew 7:12). A good parent listens to his children's "side" on issues, and rather than making authoritative commands reasons with them, explaining his reasons for his decision. He does not pull rank and say, "You are doing such and so *because I say so!*"

In the marriage ceremony a man promises to cherish and keep his wife in his love and thoughts for all time. When a husband fails to treat his wife fairly and considerately, is he fulfilling his marital pledge that he made to his wife, before God? It is a serious thing to break a vow. On the other hand, the wife should not take advantage of her husband's love by making unreasonable demands (for example, asking him to buy expensive clothing or furniture they cannot afford). Many conflicts in a marriage are caused by a wife's overspending to obtain material comforts she really does not need.

The husband should not come between his wife and what she feels to be her Christian responsibility. He would be completely out of his domain were he to attempt to do this, for his authority does not extend to her relationship with God. He may explain things to her and try to help her see what he believes to be her Christian duty. But once she has prayed and searched the Word and decided that a certain course is God's leading in her life, he should not interfere. But if he does oppose her, she should realize this is fruit of his old Adamic nature. She should be as kind and gentle with him as she can. Many Christians have endured criticism and persecution. She will find God's grace sufficient for whatever she must bear.

The husband should accompany his wife and children to the house of God as often as he can. When he cannot attend because of other duties, he should encourage them to attend without him. He has no right to discourage or forbid his wife or children from attending church or performing any other Christian duties which they feel they must perform.

Not only is it the responsibility of the husband to provide food, clothing, shelter, and the necessities of life for his family; it is also his duty to shield them from all threats of danger to their welfare. This includes physical, moral and social dangers. He should be primarily concerned for their spiritual welfare.

God holds the husband responsible to read God's Word to his family and to pray with them. If he neglects to do this, God will deal firmly with him. He will be held responsible for withholding good advice and failing to set a good example, for the lack of which his children may become involved in evil practices.

Even though his unsaved wife may never turn to God and may be a stumbling block to him, the husband will still be held accountable for any Christian responsibilities he neglected. He may even be held accountable to some extent for his wife's failure to become a Christian. Had he been faithful, perhaps she would have followed his leading and turned to God with him. It is true, of course, that each individual must answer to God for himself or herself and that none can answer for another; yet it is also true that we will not only be judged for our bad influence over others, but also for the lack of good influence we could have had on others had we been what we should have been as Christians. This is a serious thought that should be considered solemnly.

When the Husband Is Not a Christian

If the husband and father of the family is not a Christian, does not love God or try to keep his commandments, and fails to fulfill his Christian responsibilities, he forfeits his position as spiritual leader and Christian head of the home.

He cannot function in the capacity of spiritual leader. Just as "the Lord hath torn the kingdom of Israel from [Saul] this day" (1 Samuel 15:28), because of sin, so the husband can conduct himself so as to forfeit his position and be removed by God from his place as the leader of the home. If he is not a Christian, it is evident that he cannot be the spiritual leader the home needs. If he is not a man of high morals, good character, and unimpeachable life, he is not fit to be the moral and social leader of his family. He has abdicated his position and is a wanderer away from God, away from the highest and best in life. He is not worthy of being imitated or followed by his family. He is a pitiful sight in the eyes of the Lord.

The unsaved husband is unable to understand spiritual things (1 Corinthians 2:14), "dead in trespasses and sins" (Ephesians 2:1), "alienated from the life of God" (Ephesians 4:18), and "not subject to the law of God" (Romans 8:7). Consequently, he is in a poor position to do anything spiritually for his children. He is still held morally responsible, however, for the sin of being in such a state, for he is what he is by his own choosing. He could turn to Christ as Savior, assume his responsibility to God and his family, and become the spiritual leader in his home. But he must make the choice.

It is a most regrettable circumstance for any woman to be married to a man who cannot, because of his unbelief or waywardness, assume spiritual leadership in the home. When this is the case, then the wife has certain duties which fall upon her and which she must shoulder herself. We will note these in the following chapter, along with her other responsibilities.

It is not my intention to be unduly stern with

the unsaved husband of a Christian wife, but as a follower of Jesus I must "speak the truth in love" (Ephesians 4:15).

God wants the husband and father to be the spiritual, moral, and social head of his home; and he cannot toss out his responsibilities and go scot-free from the consequences. Although he has never been and may never be a Christian, God will hold him responsibile for shirking his duties. We will not only be judged for our sins of commission, but for our sins of omission as well. Jesus tells us, "And this is the condemnation, that light is come into the world, and men loved darkness rather than light, because their deeds were evil" (John 3:19). And he says of the sins of omission, "He that believeth not is condemned already, because he hath not believed in the name of the only begotten Son of God" (John 3:18). The Apostle James adds, "To him that knoweth to do good, and doeth it not, to him it is sin" (James 4:17).

Consider the story of the man in Matthew 25:24-30, who was given one talent and did not use it. Note that this man did not do any evil thing with this talent; he simply did nothing with it, except to bury it. He neither stole it, nor gave it away—he simply hid it, then returned it to his lord. Many husbands and fathers are doing just this with their talents for spiritual growth in the home. They do not use their talents for evil; they simply do not use them at all. They do not take a stand against God; they simply ignore him. They do not work against the church and its causes; they simply ignore it, stay away from it, do nothing about it. They do not object to prayer and Bible reading and good Christian counsel for their wife and children; they just don't want it for themselves. They imagine that God will let them off because they didn't oppose or reject spiritual things. They think they are neutral, neither for nor against.

What does Jesus say about this? "He that is not with me is against me; he that gathereth not with me scattereth abroad" (Matthew 12:30). In other words, if one does not take a definite stand *for* Christ as one of his faithful followers, he is taking a stand *against* him.

What happened to the man who did nothing with his talent? "Take, therefore, the talent from him, and give it unto him who hath ten talents. And cast the unprofitable servant into outer darkness; there shall be weeping and gnashing of teeth" (Matthew 25:28, 30).

What a terrible judgment came to that poor servant for his sin of *neglect*! We are not told that he did one evil deed. Not one time did he swear, refuse to attend church, or beat his wife. Yet, for neglecting his responsibility he was cast into outer darkness. "That was unfair!" you may be thinking. But God is a righteous Judge and always acts in fairness. Who are we to question his ways and his judgments, to attempt to discredit his laws? To refuse to do what we know God wants us to is a much more serious sin than we have probably ever imagined.

By the way, what was the talent which the servant had hidden and left unused? It was a sum of money which he was to use in trading to increase its value. He could have placed it in the bank, but instead he buried it. It represented something of value which could be used to produce something else of even greater value. Every person has something precious which he can use to bring increase and to assist others in life. Every person has at least one talent. That one talent may be his *influence*. No matter how weak the personality or narrow the sphere of activity, each of us has *influence*. Often it is quite silent, and yet incredibly potent.

A father walking from his house in new snow heard his little son mumbling something behind him as the child tried to step into each of his father's large footprints. Turning, he heard the boy saying, "Daddy, I'm walking right in your tracks!" Shocked and afraid as he thought of the serious consequences of his little son "walking right in your tracks," he turned his footsteps toward God and became a Christian.

A parent cannot shirk his God-given responsibility of being both an example and a teacher of his children in the things of God. Nor can he dodge the responsibility he has to be an example of righteousness and a teacher of the things of God for his wife. To attempt to dodge or deny such awesome duties is to invite the severe judgment of God.

Some time ago I laid my hand on a young man's arm and asked him about his relationship to God. He said he had quit church some eight years ago; he didn't bother to go at all any more. I said to him, "Young man, you will not go to Hell for lying, stealing, and running around with bad women." He looked at me, almost shocked at what I had said. Then I added the real punch line, the awful truth. "You will go to Hell not for all those other sins, but for *rejecting Jesus Christ, God's Son, the only remedy for sin.*"

Unsaved husbands and fathers are not going to be damned for all eternity for wife-beating, child abuse, drinking, cheating on their wives, or their other sins. They will be lost because they *rejected Christ as Savior and Lord.* This sin is above all other sins. Jesus said, "He that believeth not is condemned already, because he hath not believed in the name of the only begotten Son of God" (John 3:18). Whether or not you oppose him, if you reject him you have absolutely no hope of avoiding eternal damnation.

Every unsaved husband and father should consider this truth and think solemnly of the future punishment that awaits the sinner who rejects Christ. "It is a fearful thing to fall into the hands of the living God" (Hebrews 10:31).

If you are unsaved and reading these words, be assured that I am not apathetic about your welfare. On the contrary, it is because I am deeply concerned about you that I have written so plainly. As the husband of a Christian wife, you have seen and know the truth of God. It is a perilous thing for you to refuse to yield your heart and life to Christ.

As a man married to a Christian wife, you cannot claim ignorance. Christ Jesus himself said, "And that servant, who knew his lord's will, and prepared not himself, neither did according to his will, shall be beaten with many stripes. But he that knew not, and did commit things worthy of stripes, shall be beaten with few stripes. For unto whomsoever much is given, of him shall much be required; and to whom men have committed much, of him they will ask the more" (Luke 12:47, 48).

As a Christian, I must warn you of what your future holds. I find no verse in the Bible where God says we are to make it *easy* on sinners. God himself says, "The way of transgressors is hard" (Proverbs 13:15). "God is angry with the wicked every day. If he turn not, he will whet his sword; he hath bent his bow and made it ready. He hath prepared for him the instruments of death" (Psalm 7:11-13). "The wicked shall be turned into hell, and all the nations that forget God" (Psalm 9:17). "The Lord preserveth all those who love him, but all the wicked will he destroy" (Psalm 145:20).

Jesus said that he will tell sinners at the judgment day, "Depart from me, ye cursed, into everlasting fire, prepared for the devil and his angels" (Matthew 25:41). The very last words of Revelation concerning sinners are, "For outside are dogs, and sorcerers, and fornicators, and murderers, and idolaters, and whoever loveth and maketh a lie" (Revelation 22:15). "Dogs" means all unsaved persons, those of wicked character, whoever is outside the kingdom of God.

The sinner deserves judgment for his wickedness, stubbornness, and rebellion. His only hope is to ask for mercy and forgiveness through Jesus Christ.

Perhaps we Christians have pampered and excused unbelievers too much. Perhaps if we gave the message to them plainly, as God has done, and stopped overlooking their sins, we would come nearer winning them to God. One Christian woman prayed and wept over her unsaved husband for years, but to no avail. He heard all her prayers and still went on living in sin. Her pastor said, "Stop praying for him where he hears you." She did. Before long he asked why she didn't pray for him any more. "Why should I pray for you? You don't appreciate it. You are not turning to God. It is useless to waste any more time praying for you!" It hit him like a proverbial ton of bricks. He thought, "If she doesn't pray for me, then I may be lost forever. I had better start praying for myself!" Soon he came to church with her and was blessedly saved.

God judges sin, but he also speaks lovingly to the sinner: "Come now, and let us reason together, saith the Lord: though your sins be as scarlet, they shall be as white as snow; though they be red like crimson, they shall be as wool. If ye be willing and obedient, ye shall eat the good of the land" (Isaiah 1:18, 19). "Seek ye the Lord while he may be found, call ye upon him while he is near; let the wicked forsake his way, and the unrighteous man his thoughts, and let him return unto the Lord, and he will have mercy upon him; and to our God, for he will abundantly pardon" (Isaiah 55:6, 7).

Jesus said,

> "Come unto me, all ye that labor and are heavy laden, and I will give you rest. Take my yoke upon you, and learn of me; for I am meek and lowly in heart, and ye shall find rest unto your souls" (Matthew 11:28, 30). "For God so loved the world, that he gave his only begotten Son, that whosoever believeth in him should not perish, but have everlasting life" (John 3:16).

And he adds as a special offer,

> "For God sent not his Son into the world to condemn the world, but that the world through him might be saved" (John 3:17).

Christ's last invitation in Revelation is for the sinner too:

> "And the Spirit and the bride say, Come. And let him that heareth say, Come. And let him that is athirst come. And whosoever will, let him take of the water of life freely" (Revelation 22:17).

How much more kind and loving could God possibly be to the sinner than this? The same

God who has made it so hard on the unrepentant sinner makes it as easy as can be for the sinner who is ready to come to the Lord for mercy and pardon.

If you are unsaved, come to Christ today and be saved. Start today to live a new life in Christ. It will mean more happiness and joy, less pain and sorrow and more usefulness in your life than ever before.

4

God's Guidelines for the Wife

Wives, submit yourselves unto your own husbands, as unto the Lord. (Ephesians 5:22)

In the same manner, ye wives, be in subjection to your own husbands that, if any obey not the word, they also may without the word be won by the behavior of the wives, while they behold your chaste conduct coupled with fear. (1 Peter 3:1, 2)

I will, therefore, that the younger women marry, bear children, rule the house, give no occasion to the adversary to speak reproachfully. (1 Timothy 5:14)

. . . aged women . . . that they may teach the young women to be sober-minded, to love their husbands, to love their children, to be discreet, chaste, keepers at home, good, obedient to their own husbands, that the word of God be not blasphemed. (Titus 2:3-5)

Several state legislatures have recently introduced bills which would put marriage on a contract basis. If such a bill were to become national law, the marriage contract would be short-term and renewable only by consent of both husband and wife.

The Bible, the Christian's *marriage manual*, states clearly that God never intended marriage to be a short-term contract. It is a lifetime commitment, a permanent relationship, "till death do us part," as the traditional vow says. The sacred permanence of marriage must be protected at all costs.

As Christians, we need in-depth understanding of God's intentions for marriage. In Ephesians 5:22, we see one of the basic guidelines for the wife's attitude toward her husband. This verse is a seed-bed for the Christian home, solid ground upon which the home can be built. What are the responsibilities of the wife toward her husband?

When the Wife Is a Christian

Submission to the husband may at first seem difficult for the new wife. The Christian wife with an unsaved husband may fear that he will take advantage of her position and push her beyond what she is able to bear if she meekly submits to his every wish. But she is not to submit to his *every wish*, but only "as unto the Lord." That is the key. If her husband demands anything that she cannot do *as unto the Lord,* she is not required by God to submit to him.

However, this little phrase must not be used to dodge responsibility by saying a certain thing is not "as unto the Lord" when really she just doesn't feel like submitting. When misused, this phrase can become a tool of Satan, a snare for the wife as well as a hindrance to her mate's ever being won for God. It is only in those things in which her Christian conscience would be rightly violated that she is not to submit to him. If, for instance, he urges her to lie, or to steal, or to do something immoral, she would be wrong to comply with his wishes. For her husband to expect such actions would be to ignore the rights that are hers as a person made in God's image.

In every other phase of living—that is, when she can submit as unto the Lord—she should lovingly do so, not only for her husband's sake, but for her own as well.

In 1 Peter 3:1, the Greek word translated in the King James Version, "be in subjection," literally means "to stand under." Phillips renders it, "Adapt yourselves to your husbands," while the *New English Bible* has it, "Accept the authority of your husbands." This does not mean a tyrant-slave relationship, but it does mean that the wife is to willingly abide by her husband's final decisions concerning the family and the home—if those decisions are in accordance with God's teachings.

In *What Every Wife Should Know,* Ray C. Stedman points out that biblical submission by the wife is necessary for three reasons: First, so that the *husband may be a man in his house.* His first responsibility in the home is to provide intelligent, spiritual leadership. There cannot be two heads to anything—family, business or government—and still be successful. One figure must have the final say. A husband's true manliness begins to emerge as he takes his position as the head of his wife and home.

Submission is also a means for the *wife to display her womanhood*. Just as God created the man for leadership, he created the woman for the honorable role of wife and mother in the home. This does not mean that she is a second-class citizen, or an inferior person in any sense, but that she must cooperate with her husband's leadership in matters concerning home and family. God made Eve from a bone from Adam's side, to be with him as a "help meet" (or fit or sufficient) for him.

The masculine feminist with her mannish manners and dress is a poor demonstration of true womanhood. This does not mean that the married woman cannot work or tend a business often led by men, nor that she is in any way to be dominated by the man. But she is to go along with her husband's leadership in all matters that pertain to their lives together.

Third, this submissiveness should be in imitation of Jesus Christ. First Peter 1:1 says it is to be done "in the same manner," which refers us back to Chapter 2. There we read about Jesus Christ being in subjection to the Father in the circumstances in which the Father had placed him.

We could also refer to the Old Testament, where we see Sarah, Abraham's wife, calling him "lord" or "master." These are two examples of godly submission.

In *Unequally Yoked Wives,* Dr. C. S. Lovett has some advice for wives of unsaved husbands.[2] His "nutcracker technique" is unique and worthy of consideration. Just as the nutcracker has two main prongs between which the nut is placed and which squeeze down on the nut in order to crack it, so there are two major things a wife can do about her unsaved husband.

First, do everything in your power to be guided by the Holy Spirit in every phase of your life. Become filled with the Spirit of love, grace, and holy power. Live constantly with one main thing in view—pleasing God and winning your husband to Christ. This is letting the "light so shine before men, that they may see your good works, and glorify your Father, who is in heaven" (Matthew 5:16).

Second, when you submit to your husband in anything, gently let him know that you are doing so because you believe Jesus would want you to. If you are a good wife, it is because Jesus has made you into one. Do not belabor this in every little detail, but where there has been a difference of opinion on your part, let him know Christ makes all the difference.

For example, suppose he *demands* that you stay home from church on Sunday morning. Pray about it, and if you feel that you can stay home and not grieve the Lord, then tell your husband, "Honey, I'm staying home with you today because the Lord says the wife is to be subject to her husband. I have prayed about this and feel that at least for today I can stay with you, to please you. I am here by the Lord's permission. Perhaps you will go to church with me next Sunday."

Practice this technique without nagging, with charm and grace, letting him know that Jesus is the reason you want to be the best wife you can be.

You see, by living the life before him as one prong of the nutcracker, and giving Christ the credit for being the other prong, you will soon have him in a love-grip for God. He will either yield and go along with you, or rebel altogether and stop making demands on you. Dr. Lovett suggests that you be sure to keep your act together, reminding him now and then that if it were not for Jesus in your life you might be a real shrew! Let him see that it is Jesus in you who makes you kind and loving; who makes you a good sex partner, a good mother to your children, a good daughter-in-law to your husband's parents. Make your husband glad to be home with you. Cook his favorite foods. Make your home a pleasant place to be. Keep yourself attractive. Let him know that he is important to you. But most of all, let him know that it is Jesus who is helping you be the wife you know you should be. Let your wifely light shine, that you may be able to win him to God.

Sometimes wives ask where to draw the line.

They wish to submit, but there are some areas in which they do not feel that they can do so without violating their Christian conscience. Dr. Lovett has answered such wives very sensibly as follows:

> "God does not require any wife to give total obedience to her husband. Total obedience belongs to God alone. . . . The last thing I would counsel is complete obedience to an unregenerate man. I am satisfied that the Christian wife should give some submission in 'all things,' but total submission—never! Certainly she should not exalt the wishes of a heathen husband over those of her Lord. This is unthinkable!"[3]

He further suggests that no one can know the heart of an unsaved partner. He may demand submission in any form—from the most mild kind, which he has the right to expect, to the most disgusting sex acts, or even outright violations of God's Word. Therefore, blind total obedience is not feasible. Within the confines of civilized, normal, happy relationships between the husband and wife, her submission as long as it is pleasing to God makes both the home and life together far happier.

Lovett suggests that when a wife finds that she must refuse a husband, she might use some such approach as this:

> "Honey, as you know I am doing my best to be a submissive wife because the Lord asks me to. That means I am actually trying to please two people,

you and the Lord Jesus. Now sometimes what pleases one does not please the other and I have to make a decision. Since I have to live with him forever and I will only be with you a short time, I must refuse what you ask. I am really sorry to disappoint you, dear, but you can see when you put me in a place where I have to choose between you and Christ, I am forced to please him, although I know it disappoints you. I'm sorry it's that way, but the Lord is the one to whom I must finally give account for my life."[4]

Paul states that it is his wish that the "younger women marry, bear children, rule the house, give no occasion to the adversary to speak reproachfully" (1 Timothy 5:14).

One of the major duties of the wife is to *keep the home in such a state as to be enjoyable and pleasant* for the husband and children. A home does not have to be a *Better Homes and Gardens* showroom. It need not even have carpets on the floors or other luxuries. It may be a poor home with only the barest necessities for housekeeping. But it can be kept clean and inviting, a comfortable place for husband and children (who of course must help make it that way). It requires little in the way of expense to keep a house clean and tidy. Certainly, the house should be a good place for the children to play, especially in winter when they cannot get outdoors much. It should not be kept in department store window order and so make the family feel uncomfortable. It should not, though, be allowed to become unsanitary and messy from long neglect either. It should be clean and inviting—a place where the family can enjoy themselves without feeling either embarrassed or ashamed when company comes.

The wife should assist her husband in the religious training and care of the children. When a time has been determined for devotions with the children, either morning or evening, the wife should free herself from household duties so she can assist her husband and participate in this special worship time. If the husband's hours of employment prevent him from carrying on his duties as teacher, guide, and leader in family devotions, then it becomes the wife's duty to assume this role.

Mrs. Susanna Wesley, the mother of John Wesley, set apart one hour each week for the special teaching and training of each of her children when they were growing up in the home. While their father was a minister—and a very busy one at that—religious education and development of Christian character in the children were largely Mrs. Wesley's responsibility.

The wife is to be a warm, responsive and loving companion to her husband. Love-making and the marriage relationship are very important to the well-being of both husband and wife. To neglect this is to invite trouble into the marriage and the home.

Paul told couples that they were to "Defraud ye not one the other, except it be with consent for a time, that ye may give yourselves to fasting

and prayer; and come together again, that Satan
tempt you not for your incontinency" (or uncon-
trolled sexual desires) (1 Corinthians 7:5). Many
a wife needs to read this Scripture over many
times until it is fixed in her mind as a part of her
God-given responsibility to her husband. Husbands need to do likewise. More than this, they
need to put it into action. The American Insti-
tute, Los Angeles, California, claims that "Eigh-
ty-five percent of all divorces are caused by the
breakdown in tender love-making relationships."

The *New American Standard Bible* further clar-
ifies the passage in 1 Corinthians 7:2-5:

> But because of immoralities, let each man have his
> own wife, and let each woman have her own hus-
> band. Let the husband fulfill his duty to his wife,
> and likewise also the wife to her husband. The wife
> does not have authority over her own body, but the
> husband does, and likewise also the husband does
> not have authority over his own body, but the wife
> does. Stop depriving one another, except by agree-
> ment for a time that you may devote yourselves to
> prayer, and come together again lest Satan tempt
> you because of your lack of self-control.

Thus, we see that marriage should fulfill both
the husband's and wife's sexual needs. In marriage, each person forfeits control of his body to
his mate, and both are forbidden to refuse to
meet his or her mate's sexual needs. God is the
author of the marriage act, and it is sacred in his
eyes.

Redbook magazine recently published a summary on sexual pleasure in which 100,000 women were surveyed by Robert J. Levin. A significant finding was that "sexual satisfaction is related significantly to religious belief. With notable consistency, the greater the intensity of a woman's religious convictions, the likelier she is to be highly satisfied with the sexual pleasures of marriage." Thus, we see that Christian marriage has the greatest potential for happiness, even sexually.

In correcting the children, there should be full cooperation between the parents. The matter of discipline should not be left totally to either parent, but should be shared as equally as possible. This makes for the best relationship of the parents and for the greatest benefit to the children. A wife should not save up problems that occur during the day with the ominous threat, "Wait until your father comes home!" The child, dreading to see his father come home that night, pictures him as some kind of a disciplinary giant to be feared.

When either parent neglects his share of this responsibility, he is asking for trouble. Contrary to some parents' ideas about this, children do not appreciate the parent who is "soft" on them and allows them to get by without proper parental correction. On the contrary, they tend to appreciate the parent who is strong and consistent in correction, and may come to disrespect (if not dislike) the parent who neglects his disciplining duty. It is important that parents be consistent in their discipline. They should stand solidly together on such matters. When one parent says "No," the other should back him up and say no also.

When the husband fails in his duty to God and his children, the responsibility of Christian training for the children then becomes the duty of the Christian wife. If he wishes at times to assist her and is not hostile toward biblical truth, he should be encouraged to participate.

In instances where the husband becomes openly opposed and does not want to permit the wife to have devotions or to read the Bible to the children or teach them Christian truths, what is the Christian wife to do? Where does this place her in reference to her being submissive to her husband?

The following illustration is pertinent. No state has the right to make or enforce any law which is contrary to the Constitution of the United States or to any federal law. Likewise, the wife's first loyalty is to God and his laws; she is subject to her husband only when she may be so without violating God's law. She is to submit to him only so long as she does not spurn her higher relationship as a servant of God, nor violate her conscience in spiritual or Christian principles.

God's law commands parents to teach their children his ways. This necessitates giving children a moral example, as well as teaching them to worship. When the husband refuses to carry

out this order from God, it becomes the duty of
the wife and mother to carry it out by teaching
and praying with the children.

The wife should try in every way to avoid a
confrontation with her husband in this matter.
Let her plead her cause as effectively as she can;
but if he refuses to allow her to give the children
Christian instruction, she should follow whatever course the Spirit shows her through her
conscience.

Regarding attendance at church and her
observance of other Christian duties, the wife
should first urge her husband to go with her to
the services. If he refuses, then it becomes her
responsibility to go without him and to take her
children with her. She must not nag at her husband, but rather assure him now and then that
she would be glad to have him go with her to the
house of God. Otherwise, she should allow him
to go his own way until God brings him to his
senses and turns him toward himself. Most im-
portantly, she must pray for him daily and live a
consistent Christian life and witness before him.

In every relationship the Christian wife should
be as kind and gentle as possible. She should go
the "extra mile" whenever she can possibly do
so. Being a congenial companion will have great
effect on her unbelieving mate.

The Christian wife must not permit herself to
become discouraged because of her mate's unsaved condition, but rather keep trusting God to
save him.

The following excerpts come from a letter from a Christian wife who has lived with an unsaved husband for years. May her comments be an encouragement to you:

> For a time I felt sorry for myself. I thought I was experiencing the most terrible thing that could come into a Christian's life—being married to an unbeliever! Then God spoke to me and all began to change.

She goes on to say that she had been saved for five years when she wrote her letter. She has learned to say, "Thank you, Lord, because I've not had to go through what others have." Angered over her religion, her husband demanded that she see a psychologist. Their home nearly broke up. He would ridicule her before friends, curse and swear at her. "But the Lord becomes more precious to me day by day," she writes.

She closes her letter by saying she is not alone in her struggle, and now leads a prayer group of some ten ladies who have unsaved husbands.

The Christian married to the unbeliever walks a lonely road and faces many cheerless days and nights. But there are many benefits, too, for the Christian to enjoy on his lonesome way: knowing he is right with God; death holding no terror for him or her; confidence that his/her children can walk in God's way safely. The Christian wife knows that God is on her side, whatever may come, and there is safety in her way of life. Truly she can sing:

> Singing I go along life's way,
> Praising the Lord, praising the Lord;
> For Jesus has lifted my load.

Self-pity, the worst of all enemies, must be avoided. It has no place in true Christian living. Look instead to the hills of God, "from whence cometh my strength and blessing." Attune your ear to God's heavenly messages, which come through prayer and obedience and rejoicing in the Lord.

When the Wife Is Not a Christian
Solomon in his day said, "It is better to dwell in the wilderness than with a contentious and an angry woman" (Proverbs 21:19). "It is better to dwell in a corner of the housetop, than with a brawling woman in a wide house" (Proverbs 21:9).

Sometimes the contentious, unhappy, unruly wife can seem to be a problem beyond any solution. Often, too, such women may profess the grace of Christ and yet go right on living in their carnal, cantankerous ways.

Recently a pastor wrote on behalf of a minister whose wife has admitted to living in adultery with a member of their church. She is reading her Bible and praying much more than she ever did before. But she continues to sleep with this man in this sinful alliance. Her conscience is evidently "seared with a hot iron," as Paul referred to certain cases, and she goes on her way, blindly thinking all will turn out well. What a rude awakening awaits her sin-blinded soul. *God will not be mocked!*

Some time ago I counseled with a dear brother minister whose wife has become one of his greatest problems. She is an intelligent woman, a good leader in the church, but she treats him like so much rubbish under her feet. She has become foolishly attached to a young college-age man in his early twenties. She claims he is nothing more than a "son" in the gospel to her. She bakes him cookies and cakes and sends them to him at college. She also sends him loving cards and endearing messages chosen just for him, and regularly writes him letters which her husband is not permitted to see. On occasions when the young man is home from college, she always manages to spend time in his home with his family. When they are riding in the car, she sits between him and his mother in the front seat. They sometimes lie on the floor and play games, and she moons over him like a silly, love-sick teenaged girl.

There is no harm and often much good when older Christians befriend the young in wholesome mother-son or father-daughter relationships. But when such a relationship descends to a carnal level, untold damage is done both to the older person and to the younger.

The minister husband in this case became so exasperated that he threatened to divorce his wife for her foolishness. When she did cooperate with him in love-making, it was a cold lifeless act, merely so she could say she had given him sexual satisfaction. Such hypocritical actions are an abomination both to God and man.

I counseled this dear brother to hold on in patience and try to win her. But as a pastor of a growing charge, his is a heavy burden to bear. I have prayed for this carnal woman many times, that God will convict her of her sinful ways and help her to straighten out her life, that she might be the Christian wife she should be. Only the mercy and help of God will be able to save this marriage from shipwreck and ruin if she continues her sinful way.

I have counseled many men whose wives have been more or less of this type. Only God's grace can help a man through such a situation. (Of course, there are also many, if not more, cold perfidious husbands.) The Christian counselor must face squarely all life situations without revealing his inner feelings of shock, in order to help find possible solutions to such difficult problems.

A historic case of a contentious, rebellious wife involved John Wesley. One of England's most illustrious personalities in the eighteenth century, Wesley was a great preacher of the Word and the founder of the Methodist church. When John was a young man newly out of Oxford, he dated a lovely lady who was a fine Christian. But his older brother, Charles, who served as John's self-appointed watchdog and guardian, did not approve of the relationship. He felt she was not the one for John and never ceased interfering until he broke them up.

Later in life, John met a widow who at the beginning of their relationship professed the grace of God and displayed great admiration for the Wesleys. John married her, with Charles's approval. But she turned out to be anything but a helpful companion. She was a shrew, ill-tempered, a scolder, and a constant nagger. Her initial affection for her husband was short-lived.

When talking with the curator of the Wesley Museum, located beside the famous Wesley Chapel in London, England, I asked him, "Why did no one ever write a life story of Mrs. Wesley?" He laughed and said, "There was nothing worthwhile to write about her."

It has been reported that Mrs. Wesley would often sell some of John's favorite books while he was away on a preaching mission. Sometimes when Wesley was preaching and she was in the audience, she would yell out and contradict him or otherwise disrupt the service. On one such occasion, John Wesley said, "I have been accused of every sin in the catalog but getting drunk." His wife yelled out from the back of the auditorium, "Why, John Wesley, you know you were drunk just last week!"

John Wesley didn't stop preaching. He merely

replied, "Thank God, that completes the catalog!" and went right on with his sermon as though nothing had happened. (See *The Journal of John Wesley.*[5])

John Wesley reportedly weighed, on the average, about 122 pounds during most of his adult life. He was short of stature (about five feet, two inches tall). On one occasion, Mrs. Wesley became very angry with him. Being larger than he was, she grabbed him by his hair and dragged him around the room. Wesley reacted calmly, never laying a hand on her to avenge himself. What composure of spirit, what holiness of heart and life he demonstrated! This is an example of the grace of God working in a human heart, cleansing, empowering and saving to the utmost all who will come to God by Jesus Christ.

Abraham Lincoln's wife, Mary Todd, was a proud, haughty, ill-tempered woman. Whatever grace and religion she professed, she revealed little evidence of it on numerous occasions. She was also a spendthrift. When President Lincoln was assassinated, he was on the verge of bankruptcy because of her outrageous spending.

Lincoln's patience with his "dear Mary" was often apparent. At a dinner function in the White House dining room, she became exasperated and threw a cup of coffee in the President's face. Then she fled from the table without a word of explanation or apology. Mr. Lincoln wiped the coffee off his suit and face and said quietly, "Please excuse my Mary. She gets a little upset sometimes." Although doubtlessly embarrassed, he made no further explanation or apology. His response may have been the understatement of the century.

True wifely submission stands in marked contrast to the ugly carnal attitude of some wives. A look at the "virtuous woman" of Proverbs 31 gives an inspiring portrait of the wife's role at its highest.

> Who can find a virtuous woman? For her price is far above rubies. The heart of her husband doth safely trust in her, so that he shall have no need of spoil. She will do him good, and not evil, all the days of her life. She seeketh wool, and flax, and worketh willingly with her hands. She is like the merchants' ships; she bringeth her food from afar. She riseth also while it is yet night, and giveth food to her household, and a portion to her maidens. She considereth a field, and buyeth it; with the fruit of her hands she planteth a vineyard. She girdeth her loins with strength, and strengtheneth her arms. She perceiveth that her merchandise is good; her lamp goeth not out by night. She layeth her hands to the spindle, and her hands hold the distaff.
> She stretcheth out her hand to the poor; yea, she reacheth forth her hands to the needy. She is not afraid of the snow for her household; for all her household are clothed with scarlet. She maketh herself coverings of tapestry; her clothing is silk and purple. Her husband is known in the gates, when he sitteth among the elders of the land. She maketh fine linen, and selleth it, and delivereth girdles unto the merchant. Strength and honor are her clothing, and she shall rejoice in time to come.

She openeth her mouth with wisdom, and in her tongue is the law of kindness. She looketh well to the ways of her household, and eateth not the bread of idleness. Her children rise up, and call her blessed; her husband also, and he praiseth her. Many daughters have done virtuously, but thou excellest them all. Favor is deceitful, and beauty is vain, but a woman who feareth the Lord, she shall be praised. Give her of the fruit of her hands, and let her own works praise her in the gates.

As a Christian wife, determine to serve God faithfully in your marriage. Live out Christ's Word. Imitate the Christian examples given to us in the lives of New Testament women. Follow the footsteps of Mary Magdalene, Mary the mother of Jesus, Lydia of Philippi, Dorcas of Joppa, and others. "Seeing we are compassed about with so great a cloud of witnesses, let us lay aside every weight, and the sin which doth so easily beset us, and let us run with patience the race that is set before us" (Hebrews 12:1).

I am including a section from my book, *Happiness and Harmony in Marriage*[6] in these pages. It is intended as an encouragement to Christian wives who must often be totally responsible for giving their children Christian training and education in the home.

This section is not intended to detract from or belittle whatever advice and counsel the unsaved husband may give to his sons and daughters. It is not meant to say that their instruction is never good for their children. But the Scripture tells us that the unconverted are "dead in trespasses and in sins" (Ephesians 2:1). Therefore, they are incapable of teaching their children as effectively as if they were born-again believers. Admittedly, good instruction for the cause of Christ can come from unsaved parents. It is possible to know some of the teachings of Christ without having received him as Savior, a head knowledge of his teaching rather than a heart knowledge of Christ as personal Savior.

The following material was prepared by a remarkable young mother who had to rear her children alone:

> One may solve such a situation by working together. Even when the children are small, there are tasks which can be performed that help to create in the child the cooperativeness needed by both the parent and the child. They can make a game of housework, cooking, and yard work. It is important for the parent and child to do things together. Not only can work draw a parent and child closer, but play also is a factor in this security. Summertime can be play time by going to parks and picnics, and cooking on the home grill. Museums and zoos are also well accepted by children and can be enjoyed by the parent as well.
>
> A parent should not try to tie the child so closely as to create a problem later in life, but rather should gently lead the child into a well-adjusted adult life. The lines of communication must remain open, and a parent must put the child foremost in his or her thoughts for happiness while maintaining his or her own identity and individuality. Respect is a prime factor here. By giving the child the needed security, respect and a cooperative spirit grow to

make a good line of communication between parent and child. It is important to let the child know you are available to listen to his thoughts and ideas as well as to answer his questions. It is very possible to have a good relationship, and this is a rewarding factor in a difficult situation.

While specific Christian training and teaching did not come into this quotation, it was implicit in the methods she outlines to be used in working with the child. The Christian parent has almost sole responsibility for the education in Christian doctrines and principles which the child should receive from both parents. This can be successfully done even by one parent—with God's help.

5

Going the Second Mile

"And whosoever shall compel thee to go a mile, go with him two." (Matthew 5:41)

"But I say unto you that ye resist not evil, but whosoever shall smite thee on thy right cheek, turn to him the other also." (Matthew 5:39)

"If any man will sue thee at the law, and take away thy coat, let him have thy cloak also." (Matthew 5:40)

Then came Peter to him, and said, Lord, how often shall my brother sin against me, and I forgive him? Till seven times? Jesus saith unto him, I say not unto thee, Until seven times; but until seventy times seven. (Matthew 18:21, 22)

Vengeance is mine; I will repay, saith the Lord. (Romans 12:19)

In New Testament times the Roman soldier had the right, according to Roman law, to compel any ordinary citizen to go a mile with him in helping him in any business of state. It was to this type of commandeering that Jesus was referring when he told his disciples that "whosoever shall compel thee to go a mile, go with him two" (Matthew 5:41).

In the matter of successfully living the Christian life with an unsaved mate, it is often necessary to go the extra mile beyond what actual duty requires. For that matter, does love ever ask what duty requires? I think not. Love goes not only the extra mile, but often three, four, five, six—many extra miles.

When we get down to the basics of true New Testament living, Christ does not require of the Christian anything that would destroy his marriage. Sometimes, however, his requirements are such that the unsaved husband or unsaved wife will not tolerate them. But the unbeliever breaks up the home, not Christ's requirements. It is most often his selfishness and determination to pull his marital partner away from Christ that brings about the break—not the obedience of the Christian to Christ's way of living.

Suppose, for example, an unsaved husband should demand that his wife remain home from church and have his dinner ready promptly at eleven o'clock every Sunday because he wants a long afternoon to spend reveling in personal pleasures. Is this a reasonable demand on the Christian wife? Should she oblige him and neglect her worship of God in her church on Sunday just to please him and satisfy his selfish whim? Any sensible husband knows the answer to this is bound to be a plain and firm *no!* Vast numbers of people don't get their Sunday dinner until twelve o'clock or after—and many of these are not even churchgoing people. The husband in this case has made a totally selfish demand, and the wife is under no moral or spiritual obligation to obey it. This would not be going the extra mile morally or spiritually, but succumbing to a childish whim on the part of an unreasonable husband!

On the other hand, the Christian wife, if she is acting in love, will not dally at church talking to this one and that one, just to see how much extra time she can consume, and so arrive home far later than necessary while the husband patiently, or impatiently, waits at home. Let her find some other time for her socializing. Her responsibility now is to be home as soon after the close of worship service as is reasonable.

However, if the illness of loved ones, or a legitimate reason such as a business trip, demands that the husband leave home early on Sunday, one can understand the reasonableness of the husband asking the wife to serve dinner so he can leave right after it is served. But just to satisfy a senseless whim, no. But of course if she is resourceful, she may be able to attend an earlier service on Sunday morning and prepare an oven or crock pot meal before going to church, so that she is able to respect her husband's desire for a brunch-hour meal. Flexibility is important for the Christian wife.

In many instances where there is no moral or Christian principle at stake, the Christian should go the extra mile as cheerfully as possible to please the unsaved mate and to live in harmony with him in the home.

The Christian husband or wife should be a warm and devoted lover and never treat the unsaved companion with coldness. Maintain harmony in living except where it simply cannot be done. Go with him or her to every place that a Christian can go conscience-free. Go without resentment. Go joyfully. Go on a moment's notice without being prevented by household chores that demand attention.

The Christian wife should see, however, that the house is kept clean and tidy, the children clean and neatly dressed, if possible, for the husband when he comes home in the evenings. She should serve his meals as nearly on time as she can and in an atmosphere of affability. She should see that the children respect him and give him proper deference. She should not discuss his faults or shortcomings with other members of the family, especially with his children. Never should she belittle him in front of his friends or peers. She should also endeavor to keep herself as attractive as possible for their evenings together. In other words, she should cushion his life with as much happiness as she can. Remember, he may have had a hard day at the office and deserves the warm, relaxed atmosphere of the home at day's end. Also, if he never turns to

God, this life is the only pleasure he may have—through all eternity.

Likewise, the Christian husband should show all the deference he can to his unsaved wife. Try in all ways to please her where it can be done without sacrificing any moral or spiritual principle. Go out of your way to make her as happy as possible. Be sure to remember her birthday and your wedding anniversary with appropriate gifts. Make life as cheerful for her as you can. Surprise her with no-occasion gifts such as books or flowers that clearly say, "I love you!" Convince her by your demonstrations of love for her that your religion does not in any way come between you.

The Christian should also show the deepest concern for the social and moral welfare of the unsaved spouse. Even though you do not attend places of worldly amusement with your spouse, try to be understanding about what he or she may encounter when there. Do your best to be as attractive as possible so that your mate may not be tempted to look to someone else for satisfaction. Involve yourself in as many of his interests as you can as a Christian. Is your mate interested in astronomy, geology, antiques? Read as widely as possible in the fields of his interest, and try to understand what he is seeking in the type of entertainment he pursues outside the home. Is it exercise, relaxation, entertainment, gourmet cooking?

The Christian must not allow herself to be

constantly criticizing the unbelieving mate for his choice of entertainment. This may be his way of enduring the boredom he finds in his work or life. Avoid criticizing his friends; he will only rise to their defense. Steer away from criticizing his reading choices also. Try to understand why he reads the type of material he does. If he or she reads sex magazines, it may be a means of vicariously satisfying a need which is not being met at home. It would be better to find out what it is that he or she wants and needs and try to meet that need, than to criticize and find fault. The wife of an unsaved husband should understand that a man's sexual needs are often greater on an average than those of the woman. She should try to meet these needs as fully as possible. It may be that a husband's frustration at not being sexually satisfied is a factor in his not being more receptive to the Christianity she professes! Read again 1 Corinthians 7:5. This verse is important to your Christian living. Get a good marriage manual, preferably written by a Christian, and endeavor to improve your sensitivity and understanding to your mate's sex needs.

The following is an explanatory examination of 1 Corinthians 7:5 from the *New Bible Commentary, Revised:*

> Marriage must be real, not "spiritual." Should give; the Greek indicates the paying of a debt rather than the conferring of a favor. Husband and wife have equal sex rights, a novelty in antiquity. Do not refuse (Greek "defraud"), i.e., withhold

what is owed. Any abstention must be mutually agreed, temporary, and have a spiritual objective (cf. 1 Peter 3:7).

Devote yourselves; literally "have leisure for." Cf. Ecclesiastes 3:5; Joel 2:15, 16. Paul's concession shows wise balance. Abstinence carried to extreme may only expose one to temptation to satisfy the appetite wrongly. Having opposed licence in 6:13-20, Paul now opposes asceticism. The two extremes were encouraged by Gnostic views of matter as evil (cf. 1 Timothy 4:3). Paul argues that marriage is the norm. Celibacy, as some say, is good. But temptation to immoral acts (the Greek is plural) abounds especially in Corinth. Marriage was the divinely appointed safeguard; so each should have (i.e., must, not may) his own spouse—an incidental reference to monogamy.[7]

In the whole matter of trying to meet the needs of the unsaved mate, remember that in his blindness *he wants you to do and be just what he wants,* regardless of your religion. Often it is really the Christ in you that he is against, more than you. If you turned to the old life of sin and went along with him to satisfy his demands, he would be most unhappy. He would then feel the guilt of causing you to turn from the Lord; hence, there would be no satisfaction in this for him.

Do everything in your power to be as good a companion as you can possibly be and to do all you can to please him, short of a compromise of spiritual things. Then leave the matter with the Lord. Trust him to fully undertake for you. Above all, do not try to impress your spouse with

your deeply religious life. Try to have your devotions all finished, for instance, at bedtime. Do
not expect him to wait for you to say your final
prayers at the bedside—do this alone before that
hour arrives. If you pray a final good night
prayer, make it brief. God understands and does
not want you to become an aggravation when it is
not necessary.

Try to live as spontaneous a life as possible, so
you won't irritate your unsaved mate with ob-
vious forced effort. Religion is a very personal
matter, and you need not try to impress your
unsaved mate with religious ceremony. He is apt
to be more impressed by your daily, victorious
living, your sweetness of disposition, your cheer-
fulness of temperament, and your readiness to
lend a helping hand whenever needed. Whatever doubts you may have about your religious experience, keep them to yourself, or share them
with another mature Christian—never with your
unbelieving mate.

Remember, your life may be the only living
witness for Christ your unsaved mate will ever
know. So try to honor God in the best way you
know how. Under all conditions, pray and think
through every problem. Do not give way to
apathy, but try in whatever ways you feel best to
be as good an example for the Lord as you possibly can. As Paul wrote, "Walk in wisdom toward
them that are outside, redeeming the time. Let
your speech be always with grace, seasoned with
salt, that ye may know how ye ought to answer

every man" (Colossians 4:5, 6).

If your unsaved mate wishes to hear about your church services or other Christian opportunities, share them with him. If he does not, then don't irritate him with details of such activities. Avoid making remarks of appreciation or special reference to persons of the opposite sex in Christian circles. This may serve to make him or her feel that you are being specially attracted to the other person. No matter how much you appreciate the pastor, for instance, constant remarks about him and his "wonderful sermons," his great kindness, etc. are apt not to serve any good purpose. Often the unbeliever tends to be jealous of you and your church relationship. Such remarks only serve to aggravate such a feeling. Remember that what you see about your pastor that makes him wonderful is really Christ in him and not his own personality. Without Christ, he would be as unpersonable as any other sinner. Exalt Christ and say little about the persons he is using in his work, and you will be better off in the long run. It is far better, for instance, to say, "The Lord blessed my soul through his Word this morning," than to say, "Our pastor's sermon was a great blessing to my soul." Let the unsaved quarrel with the Lord, and not with your reference to your pastor.

Finally, try to so live that your religion is a vitally uplifting experience, a grace in you that makes you easier to live with and a better, more congenial companion. Add an eleventh beatitude: "Blessed are those who are pleasant to live with." Take note of any criticism by which you may see how to improve yourself and your representation of Christianity, but avoid losing heart if you don't get encouragement from your unbelieving spouse. Live in peace of mind and with an undivided heart, serving the Lord joyfully and looking to him for daily guidance as to how best to win the unbeliever. If you win him or her in the end, you will have accomplished a good work. If in the end they are lost, your reward in Heaven will be based on your loyalty to God rather than on your success in seeing your mate won to Christ.

Whether you win or lose your unsaved mate, in the end your reward will be just as great one way as the other—if you have honestly done all within your power to win your mate to Christ. How good to know God does not reward us for our successes, but for our faithfulness. Jesus said, "Be thou faithful unto death, and I will give thee a crown of life" (Revelation 2:10). May we all be good servants of Christ, whether in life or in death.

(Note: I would like to recommend that the reader secure Dr. C. S. Lovett's book *Unequally Yoked Wives* and read it carefully. It may be ordered from Personal Christianity, Box 157, Baldwin Park, California 91706 for $1.95.)

6

Building a Bridge to Tomorrow

"Wherefore, they are no more two, but one flesh. What, therefore, God hath joined together, let not man put asunder." (Matthew 19:6)

For this cause shall a man leave his father and mother, and shall be joined unto his wife, and they two shall be one flesh. . . . Nevertheless, let every one of you in particular so love his wife even as himself; and the wife, see that she reverence her husband. (Ephesians 5:31, 33)

. . . If any brother hath a wife that believeth not, and she be pleased to dwell with him, let him not put her away. And the woman who hath an husband that believeth not, and if he be pleased to dwell with her, let her not leave him. For the unbelieving husband is sanctified by the wife, and the unbelieving wife is sanctified by the husband; else were your children unclean, but now are they holy. (1 Corinthians 7:12-14)

The Christ who spoke the strong words recorded in Matthew would not prescribe the breakup of a home just because one spouse is a

Christian and the other is not. He is the author of the sacred union of marriage. He never intended for any marriage to end in divorce, not even one. The legal termination of a marriage is man's idea, not God's.

One of the saddest pieces of legislation Moses ever set into motion was that giving permission for a couple to divorce. Christ said, "From the beginning it was not so. And I say unto you, Whosoever shall put away his wife, except it be for fornication, and shall marry another, committeth adultery; and whosoever marrieth her who is put away committeth adultery" (Matthew 19:8, 9).

There is no higher authority to whom we can go than Jesus Christ. He is the Supreme Court in human affairs; his is the last word. He tells us, "Moses, because of the hardness of your hearts, permitted you to put away your wives." But he adds in the next breath that this was not God's original purpose.

God says of himself, "I am the Lord, I change not" (Malachi 3:6). If God is unchanging, then his desires and laws for man must be unchanging also. He has *permitted* some things, such as divorce, but they are not his first choice, and never his pleasure. Even when conditions become so bad as to be intolerable—if the husband becomes a madman and badly beats his wife, endangering her life—God still does not want the couple to end their marriage in divorce. He wills rather that the husband repent, turn to God, and ask his wife's forgiveness, and that they make a go of their marriage together in the love of Christ. Even when a marriage is on the proverbial rocks and there is no apparent hope, if the couple—husband and wife—will turn to God, he can give grace and love and bring out of their chaos a loving and happy home molded in the marital bliss he originally intended.

Divorce occurs when one or both parties to the marriage have made up their minds that they no longer love each other and want to end their marriage. One or both have suffered the deterioration of life together, and they want an end to their unhappiness. Many times if they would listen to their common sense, they would stop fighting each other long enough to think things through and save their marriage.

Any couple which once had a happy marriage can find the same or even greater love and happiness together *if each partner is willing to go the extra mile in their relationship*. Assuredly, this could require a great deal of forgiving and forgetting past arguments and failures, *but it can be done with God's help*. Even in situations where two people have not really loved each other and had only married to solve a bad situation—for example, the girl was pregnant and they wanted to give the child legal status and a name—even that couple can *learn to love each other* and know marital happiness. It may take both a moral and psychological miracle, but nothing is impossible with God. Such miracles occur daily throughout the world and they can occur again—today, in your world.

It is my contention that if any man and woman will face all of the issues that tore them apart, forgive each other wholly, bury the past, and turn to each other with willing hearts and minds, and also ask Christ to rule in their home in a new and living way, such a couple can build a strong and healthy marriage.

Now let us consider several factors in building this bridge to tomorrow for the unequally yoked couple.

Determine that both of you are going to make a success of your marriage—whatever the difficulties. The power of united minds over a situation is incredible and little short of a miracle. Never underestimate the power of the human mind to perform unthinkable feats if it exercises determination, especially if it is in daily communion with the omnipotent God. "Faith is the substance of things hoped for, the evidence of things not seen" (Hebrews 11:1).

Set some goals to work toward. Recently the newspapers carried a story of an old gentleman and his wife in the Midwest who had lived together for seventy-nine years. When they were married at nineteen, it was part of their wedding pledge that they would *never quarrel.* The husband says they have kept this promise. When things begin to get heated between them and a quarrel seems imminent, they remember their marriage pledge and say, "Oh, pshaw, it isn't worth a quarrel!"

When you consider the real issues of life, the majority of things married couples argue about are pretty trivial. Perhaps a goal of never quarreling would be a good one for your marriage. Or you could set other goals, such as building a beautiful life together, building a home according to your dreams of what a home should be, working out a plan for retirement together, or furthering your education. Remember, if you aim at nothing, you will hit it.

Communicate; talk things over. Make up your minds that you will never permit anything to sever your relationship. Learn to resolve your conflicts with a minimum of emotion. Determine to make a success of your marriage from the start, or even the restart.

A teenaged girl who was getting married was asked by a friend, "Jeanie, are you having a church wedding?"

"Of course I am," she answered, then added, "Every girl has a church wedding for her *first* wedding!" She obviously considered divorce a valid option if her first marriage was not satisfactory. This is the death note of far too many marriages today. "If it doesn't work out, we can always get a divorce and marry someone else." This sand-foundation philosophy of life wrecks the rock-foundation of the Christian home.

Determine in your minds that though one of you is a Christian and the other is not, this is no reason for divorce. Tens of thousands of couples have gone through life unequally yoked and have remained married. Certainly you will not experience as deep a togetherness in the many rich experiences of life as you would if you were both Christians. Nor will you enjoy worldly pleasures together as you would if you were both unbelievers. But there are many wonderful things which you can enjoy in life together if you determine to do so. Not everything in your lives is either distinctly Christian, or entirely non-Christian and thus off-bounds. Most of life's happier experiences can be enjoyed together: taking vacations; going on family outings; watching the children grow through various stages to adulthood; helping them with their lessons; attendance together at school functions, community affairs, and family get-togethers; church outings. Also, hobbies such as gardening, antiques, music, art, boating, and sports activities can all prove to be enjoyable family sharing experiences that help strengthen a marriage.

Determine to deal with money matters objectively and without emotional involvement. First Timothy 6:10 tells us, "The love of money is the root of all evil." Unresolved money problems can wreak havoc in a marriage. Money management should be a joint effort, unless one partner in the marriage is much better at managing funds than the other. Such an arrangement should be by mutual agreement.

Giving money to God may be a problem if both partners in the marriage are not Christians. Pray about this, and remember that God does not ask for giving from those who have not received his Son.

"Be angry, and sin not; let not the sun go down upon your wrath" (Ephesians 4:26). The married couple that practices these words will never appear in divorce court. Settle every disagreement before bedtime, and grudges will not have a chance to become first a smouldering and then an exploding volcano, pouring the lava of accumulated angers over its rim. Paul ends his chapter with, "And be ye kind one to another, tenderhearted, forgiving one another, even as God, for Christ's sake, hath forgiven you" (Ephesians 4:32).

Share your innermost feelings about various matters with each other. Never bottle up things that can and should be shared. Share with each other the things that concern you both, but keep in your own confidence those things that are of no interest or importance to the other person. Trust each other fully, and give the other person the benefit of any doubt.

Often the unsaved spouse may be capable of more understanding and help than the Christian may think. You will never know until you try him or her. Should you, however, find him incapable of emotional support, then form Christian friendships which will help you to live your life and will not prove a hindrance to his.

Work at maintaining your marriage relationship. No marriage, however well it starts off, can be continuously happy and successful unless both parties work at keeping the relationship alive and warm. Communication cannot break down without the marriage suffering unhappy strain and stress. Marital harmony is not automatic; it must be protected and nourished. You wind up with only weeds and grasses in a garden if you do not cultivate it. Likewise, a good marriage must be cultivated and all the weeds of misunderstanding removed day by day. No marriage will succeed automatically, any more than a friendship can grow if friends do not keep in touch.

Be willing to compromise with each other where no moral or spiritual issue is at stake. Few unbelievers with Christian mates want the Christian to compromise basic scriptural issues just for them. They may not want to observe Sunday as the Lord's day, for example, but seldom ever will they ask you to compromise a solid Christian principle. Usually the unsaved mate asks for compromises in "little" matters where there is no outright moral or spiritual principle to be violated.

In most issues, the Christian needs to be sure she correctly understands the unsaved spouse's wishes. For example, missing an occasional service at church is not a compromise of a vital principle and can often be done without harm to one's Christian witness. But if the unbeliever demands giving up regular attendance at God's house, the issue is not so simple.

Learn to adjust to changes in your mate. Changes

are a part of living. Certain chemical changes in body functions can "upset the apple cart" for some persons. Perhaps a husband or wife has been warm sexually, but almost overnight becomes cool and indifferent to his or her mate's sexual needs. Has he or she lost interest in the marriage partner, or secretly fallen in love with someone else? Usually none of these factors is responsible. Certain chemical changes occurring in the body may have affected the emotional pattern of life. A medical checkup may be advisable.

Cultural patterns sometimes begin to change in one's life. For instance, often at about forty years of age, one will notice a definite change in lifestyle. It may be a good idea for both partners at this age, or even earlier, to read the popular best seller, *Passages,* a secular book which accurately describes this type of change. Among non-Christians, normal changes in the various stages of life can be particularly drastic. These will not cause divorce or crises in the home if they are understood and met properly. They can be handled if the couple has maintained good communication with each other.

Do not try to remake your spouse. Even if you are not content with some of his or her personality traits or developed habits, try to understand and accept them. If changes are to be made, do not discuss these before company or even before the children. Mention desired changes lovingly; keep your voice gentle and under control. Let love do the talking. When you do offer a criticism or suggest a change, sandwich your suggestion between two compliments.

Be generous with your compliments to your mate. When you sincerely compliment your spouse, this instantly builds up his or her self-image. It is like a refreshing shower on a hot summer afternoon.

Tolerate your spouse's faults. Tolerance is a Christian grace which at all times the Christian should manifest toward the unsaved partner in the marriage. Remember that "the flesh is weak" (Matthew 26:41), and when sin still reigns in the unbeliever's heart and life, it makes him even more subject to being overbearing and lacking in the grace needed to keep the marriage running smoothly. Even those of us who know Christ are in the process of becoming what we should be.

Set aside times to be together, just the two of you. This is just as needful after several years of marriage as it was in the early days. Remember how eagerly the new husband hurried home after work to be with his bride? Remember how you rushed dinner to have it ready on time? Remember the long, happy hours you spent in each other's arms? A little special attention now and then can still oil the otherwise squeaky marriage wheel.

One of the greatest tragedies in modern life is the way marriages are breaking up. One of the most common reasons for this is that husbands and wives do not take out time from their busy lives to be together. In other words, they are so busy making a living that they have no time to *make a life!* Jesus' words, "Beware of covetousness; for a man's life consisteth not in the abundance of the things which he possesseth," apply as well to a marriage as to an individual life.

Time together is more important than we usually realize. If you both work, as many married couples do, and have almost no time for being together, then get a baby-sitter and go out to eat occasionally. After the meal, drive to a lakeside or a park. Take time to just quietly enjoy the evening together. Don't ruin the evening by saying, "I wonder what the baby is doing," or, "I hope the children are all right." Forget the children for the time being; God intended for you and your husband to have good times alone. Learn to enjoy each other's company in all of the aspects of living together.

Seek your mate's opinion on every major thing which concerns you both. Do not try to ignore issues and interests and play dumb. This does not help your relationship with an intelligent spouse. Ignorance of family affairs can often lead to discontentment, especially in the husband. Each partner should respect and appreciate the knowledge possessed by the other.

Ask God to help you find solutions for the problems in your marriage. True religion never weakened any marriage. And the inclusion of God in every facet of life together is the most stabilizing factor that can be introduced into a marriage.

What if an unbelieving spouse insists that the Christian abandon her faith? She must then decide whether she will give up her faith in Christ or remain true to him and suffer whatever consequences may come. If the husband chooses to leave her because of this, she will at least have the satisfaction of pleasing her Savior.

Paul says that "if the unbelieving depart, let him depart. A brother or a sister is not under bondage in such cases; but God hath called us to peace" (1 Corinthians 7:15). Total desertion, such as this would doubtless be, is considered by many theologians to be sufficient ground for divorce, freeing the abandoned partner from moral obligation to the deserter.

But in most cases, the unbelieving husband will enter no objection to the wife's religion, as long as she does not neglect her duties at home for the sake of religious activities. And few unsaved wives will ever oppose their husband's Christian convictions as long as he does not neglect her for the church and its involvements.

The principles we have discussed can help you build a strong bridge to tomorrow, and strengthen your marriage with the concrete of mature Christian living.

It is good to conclude these chapters on marriage with the beautiful words of Matthew Henry:

> Eve was not taken out of Adam's head to top him, neither out of his feet to be trampled on by him,

but out of his side to be equal with him, under his arm to be protected by him, and near his heart to be loved by him.[8]

God intends marriage to be the most beautiful relationship known to man. He compares it to the relationship of his church (the bride) to his Son (the Bridegroom). It is a divinely appointed partnership that offers opportunity for spiritual growth and exploration of the joys and delights that are a part of the kingdom of God on earth.

Notes

1. Clyde Narramore, *Married to an Unbeliever* (Rosemead, Calif.: Narramore Christian Foundation).

2. C. S. Lovett, *Unequally Yoked Wives* (Baldwin Park, Calif.: Personal Christianity, 1968).

3. Lovett, *Unequally Yoked Wives*, pp. 80, 81.

4. Lovett, *Unequally Yoked Wives*, p. 82.

5. Percy L. Parker, *The Journal of John Wesley* (Chicago: Moody Press, 1974).

6. William S. Deal, *Happiness and Harmony in Marriage* (Kansas City, Mo.: Beacon Hill Press).

7. Donald Guthrie, *New Bible Commentary, Revised* (Grand Rapids, Mich.: Eerdmans, 1950).

8. Matthew Henry, *Matthew Henry's Commentary on the Whole Bible* (Grand Rapids, Mich.: Zondervan, 1966).